D0715335

The Book of
Texas Wisdom

The Book of
Texas Wisdom

Common Sense and Uncommon Genius
From 101 Texans

Compiled and Edited by Criswell Freeman

WALNUT GROVE PRESS
P.O. Box 58128
Nashville, TN 37205
(615) 256-8584

ISBN 0-9640955-8-0

The ideas expressed in this book are not, in all cases, exact quotations, as some have been edited for clarity and brevity. In all cases, the author has attempted to maintain the speaker's original intent. In some cases, material for this book was obtained from secondary sources, primarily print media. While every effort was made to ensure the accuracy of these sources, the accuracy cannot be guaranteed. For additions, deletions, corrections or clarifications in future editions of this text, please write WALNUT GROVE PRESS.

WALNUT GROVE PRESS books are available at special discounts for sales in bulk purchases, fund-raising, or educational use. For information, contact WALNUT GROVE PRESS.

Printed in the United States of America
by Vaughan Printing, Inc.
Book Design by Armour&Armour
Cover Design by Mary Mazer
Typesetting & Page Layout by Sue Gerdes
Edited by Alan Ross
1 2 3 4 5 6 7 8 9 10 • 95 96 97 98

ACKNOWLEDGMENTS
The author gratefully acknowledges the helpful support of Rona Braselton, Mary Susan Freeman, John Gerdes, Don Pippen, Carol Roark and all the writers who have recorded the lives, words and deeds of great Texans.

To My Grandmother

Marie T. Freeman

The Rose of Royce City

Table of Contents

Introduction

Texas remains, in many ways, a nation unto itself. From this diverse land springs a wisdom that combines the hospitality of the Old South, the unhurried calm of Mexico, and the gritty determination of the Wild West.

This book shares a message of hope, humor, and courage from 101 great Texans. This is not intended to be a complete collection of Lone Star quotes; that project could fill an encyclopedia. Instead, I have attempted to compile a sampling of profound yet simple thoughts that sum up the Texas spirit.

In researching this book, I discovered an overriding theme that is, for me, the hallmark of Texas wisdom. That theme is optimism. Texans don't shy away from big projects because they possess the faith to begin and the courage to endure. That's the way the state was founded; that's the way the state has prospered. If an oil well turns out to be a dry hole, there's always the next one. If yesterday's boom has gone bust, there's always tomorrow. The lesson of the Alamo is not lost: defeat need not be permanent.

Texas is unique, and Texans know it. They pride themselves on being the biggest, the boldest and the best. But this collective pride is not empty arrogance. More often than not, Lone Star braggadocio is based upon fact, not fiction. Texans possess the genius of persistence fueled by resolute optimism. First, Texans convince themselves that they can do great things. Then, they go out and do them.

Consider this book a brief introduction to the spirit of Texas — Lone Star Wisdom 101. Like the state from which it comes, that wisdom is big. Very big.

1

Texas

A cowboy died and went to heaven. When he arrived at the pearly gates, he was met by a frowning Saint Peter. The cowboy, remembering more than a few earthly indiscretions, feared the worst. But Saint Peter neither turned him away nor beckoned him in. After a few tense moments, the cowboy summoned all his courage and asked the obvious question, "Saint Peter, what's the matter?" The old saint opened his palms apologetically and said, "You can come in, but it won't be like Texas."

From the Red River to the Rio Grande, the Lone Star State is unmatched, unequaled, and unsurpassed. The following quotes confirm what Saint Peter already knew: Texas is quite a special place.

Texas is the finest
portion of the globe that
ever blessed my vision.

Sam Houston

Texas Wisdom

I must say as to what I have seen of Texas,
it is the garden spot of the world, the best
land and the best prospects for health
I ever saw, and I do believe it is
a fortune to any man to come here.

Davy Crockett

I am forced to conclude that God made
Texas on his day off, for pure entertainment,
just to prove that all that diversity could be
crammed into one section of earth
by a really top hand.

Mary Lasswell

Writers facing the problem of Texas find
themselves floundering in generalities,
and I am no exception.

John Steinbeck

Texas is neither Southern nor Western.
Texas is Texas.

William Blakley

Texas is a state of mind in the same way
that France or Russia are states of mind.
This sense of nationalism has not
disappeared, and it shows no more signs
of disappearing than in Paris or Moscow.

T. R. Fehrenbach

Texas, the twenty-eighth state to be admitted
to the Union (1845) and the only one which,
as an independent nation, came in by treaty,
derives its name from "tejas," an Indian word
meaning "friend," "friendly," or "allies."

Federal Writer's Program, 1940

Other states were carved or born.
But Texas grew from hide and horn.

Author Unknown

Texas Wisdom

Like the extrovert she is,
		Texas welcomes attention.

Mary Lasswell

Texas is a blend of valor and swagger.

Carl Sandburg

Texas is the crossroads of the world.
		Everything here is big.

Bobby Lee

Co-owner of the Big Texan Steak Ranch, Amarillo

Texas

Welcome to a country where the natives
are friendly, and the language barrier
is easily overcome. Texas!

From the official state travel map

Texas is a state of mind.
Texas is an obsession. Above all, Texas
is a nation in every sense of the word.

John Steinbeck

Texas has a reverberating quality
that other places don't have.

James Michener

Texas is the "Old Man River" of states.
No matter who runs it or what happens
politically, it just keeps rolling along.

Will Rogers

Texas Wisdom

I done drew the line. Just like at the Alamo.
You're either on one side of the line or the
other. I don't want to ever leave Texas again.
Bum Phillips

The West is not just a place.
The West is an idea. Here in the West,
we learned that man's possibilities were
as spacious as the sky that covered him.
Lyndon Baines Johnson

Texas is the most diverse of states.
The only thing we don't have is year-round
snow-capped mountain peaks. We've got
just about everything else.
Ann Richards

In Texas, the shadow of Spain is a long one.
Mary Lasswell

If you've ever driven across Texas, you know how different one area of the state can be from another. Take El Paso. It looks as much like Dallas as I look like Jack Nicklaus.

Lee Trevino

I thought I knew Texas pretty well, but I had no notion of its size until I campaigned it.

Ann Richards

Even the weeds in Texas are artistic.

Mary Lasswell

Texas is the most beautiful state in the universe.

D. D. Lewis

One Texas claim is that it doesn't have
a climate, just weather.

J. Frank Dobie

The one great inescapable fact in Texas
is the weather.

Mary Lasswell

If you don't like the weather,
wait thirty minutes and it will change.

Texas Saying

The wind blows a lot in the Texas Panhandle.
It's part of the landscape.

T. Boone Pickens

Texas one and indivisible. Remember the Alamo.

State Seal of Texas

Texas is too big a state to take in one gulp

from The Texas Monthly Guidebook to Texas

Texas could wear
Rhode Island
as a watch fob.

Pat Neff

2

Texans

Texans are different. They are, simultaneously, a part of and apart from the other 49 states. They possess a territorial pride which borders on unshakable devotion.

A story is told of a young boy who was chastised by his father for asking a stranger if he was from the Lone Star State. The father warned his son, "Never ask a man if he's from Texas. If he is, he'll tell you. If he's not, why embarrass him?"

Mother Nature has blessed the Lone Star State with a wide array of natural gifts, but the greatest treasure is neither animal, vegetable nor mineral. The following passages describe the most unique natural asset in all of Texas: Texans.

With a population descended from English, French and Germans forming the bone and sinew of our character, Texas will possess all the moral elements of greatness.

Sam Houston

Life in Texas has the leisureliness of the Old South, the manana-ness of Mexico, and the waiting quality of the Indian.

J. Frank Dobie

Texan is what you are, not what you were or might be.

Robert Ruark

I may have been born in Louisiana,
but I'll be a Texan till the day I die.

Van Cliburn

N o matter how far we may wander,
Texas lingers with us, coloring
our perceptions of the world.

Elmer Kelton

First buy a cowboy hat and boots.
Then you're on your way to being a Texan.

James Michener

Texans

I think Texans have more fun
than the rest of the world.

Tommy Tune

There was only two things the old-time
cowpunchers were afraid of:
a decent woman and being set afoot.

E.C. "Teddy Blue" Abbott

Yet, for all the facets of the Texas mind, all
the size and diversity of the state, there is
one quality that overrides all others:
the inherent hardness of the land.

John Connally

I love Texas because Texas is future-oriented,
because Texans think anything is possible.
Texans think big.

Phil Gramm

What Texans can dream, Texans can do.

George W. Bush

Texans are very competitive people.

Jack Burke, Jr.

Texans are proud of their own.

Ann Richards

I have never known anyone from Texas,
no matter how far they go or what they do,
who isn't proud of being from Texas.

Van Cliburn

Texans have always been Number One
in their own minds. There are no people as
proud of their heritage. We've got a lot to
brag about, and rightfully so.

Dick DeGuerin

Texans want to believe they're different.

James Michener

3
Hospitality

Texas has a rich history of hospitality. In its earliest days, the Lone Star State rolled out the welcome mat for hundreds of thousands of new settlers. Richard Bennett Hubbard, a 19th century governor and United States senator, noted, "Texas, with traditional hospitality, extends her warm grasp with open doors. Texas wants men, honest men, with brave hearts and strong arms to populate her wilderness."

Today, Hubbard's "traditional hospitality" lives on in Texas hearts — and even on Texas highways. The spirit of "tejas" is alive and well.

Never betray a friend or comrade
    for the sake of your own gain.

Belle Starr

Never pass up an opportunity to do
    an honorable favor for an honest friend.

Lyndon Baines Johnson

If you want to get along, go along.

Sam Rayburn

You can't get ahead
    while you're trying to get even.

Dick Armey

Nobody is perfect. Look
for the good in others.
Forget the rest.

Barbara Bush

The best public relations are based on good deeds.

Stanley Marcus

He climbs highest who helps another up.

Zig Ziglar

Whenever I meet someone, I try to imagine
him wearing an invisible sign saying,
"Make me feel important!" I respond to
the sign immediately, and it works.

Mary Kay Ash

Winning has always meant much to me,
but winning friends has meant more.

Babe Didrikson Zaharias

If we must disagree, let's disagree
without being disagreeable.

Lyndon Baines Johnson

In seeking truth, you have to get
both sides of a story.

Walter Cronkite

Fairness begets fairness, and loyalty begets
loyalty, and generosity begets generosity.
That's just the way humans live and work.

Trammell Crow

Peace and justice are two sides
of the same coin.

Dwight D. Eisenhower

Yⁱou can be so anesthetized by your own
pain that you don't fully share the
pain of someone close to you.

Lady Bird Johnson

Listening is an art.
And the first tenet of the skill is paying
undivided attention to the other person.

Mary Kay Ash

Sandwich every bit of criticism
between two heavy layers of praise.

Mary Kay Ash

Sincerely attempt to heal, on an honest
Christian basis, every misunderstanding
that you have had or now have.
Drain off your grievances.

Lyndon Baines Johnson

Hospitality in the prairie country is not
limited. Even if your enemy passes your way,
you must feed him before you shoot him.

O. Henry

Tejas

Indian word for friend

Friendship

State Motto of Texas

4

Advice

Giving advice can be a tricky thing — taking it even trickier. Indian Creek native Katherine Anne Porter once cautioned, "Never take advice, including this." Despite this warning, the following words of wisdom come courtesy of thoughtful Texans. Read them *before* deciding whether or not to take Miss Porter's advice.

I leave this rule for others when I'm dead. Be always sure you're right — then go ahead.

Davy Crockett

Dare to risk public criticism.

Mary Kay Ash

Don't follow the crowd.
Just trust your own horse and don't get
into the same rut as everybody else.

Grandfather's advice to Barbara Jordan

Conform and be dull.

J. Frank Dobie

Do not try to live up to your neighbors.
They are only interested in
their possessions, not yours.

Barbara Bush

The older I get, the more wisdom I find in
the ancient rule of taking first things first —
a process which often reduces the most
complex human problems
to manageable proportions.

Dwight D. Eisenhower

Deal with one pitch at a time and
make every one count.

Nolan Ryan

Don't ever go in someplace until you
figure how in the heck you're
gonna get yourself back out.

Red Adair

Don't count the crop till it's in the barn.

Sam Rayburn

Don't fade away.

Buddy Holly

Don't compromise yourself.
You're all you've got.

Janis Joplin

Don't talk about money. It's embarrassing
for others and quite frankly, vulgar.

Barbara Bush

Learn to remember names.

Lyndon Baines Johnson

His first rule for winning new friends

Avoid hating anyone.

Dwight D. Eisenhower

Never miss an opportunity to say
a word of congratulations.

Lyndon Baines Johnson

Drive Friendly — The Texas Way

State Welcome Sign

Try, but don't try too hard. Just try
hard enough, and things will go better.

Rodney Crowell

Be patient — it's the most important thing.

Tris Speaker

I get my advice from old men and
my motivation from young ones.

Lyndon Baines Johnson

Never be afraid to recreate yourself.

George Foreman

Let your tongue speak what your heart thinks.

Davy Crockett

If you simply tell the truth, you'll never get
mixed up. Then you don't have
to remember what you've said.

Sam Rayburn

Never forget, son, when you represent Texas,
always go first class.

James Michener

5

Boom and Bust

It seems that everything in Texas is bigger, and so it is with booms and busts. Good times in the Lone Star State can be very good; the hard times can be awful. But even during the darkest days, Texas optimism shines through.

An old-time politician was once asked about an economic recession. "Son," he replied, "We don't have recessions in Texas. But I must admit, this is the worst boom we've had in years."

When your hand is in the lion's mouth, withdraw it quickly.

Sam Houston

Defeat is something that comes from within.

Darrell Royal

No one can defeat us unless we first
defeat ourselves.

Dwight D. Eisenhower

When times get tough, you can adjust
or ... you can adjust.

Lady Bird Johnson

You never know your luck till the wheel stops.
Western Saying

In order to really appreciate the good things,
you've got to have been down.
Earl Campbell

Don't give up. You never know
what's going to happen.
Tom Landry

Never give in. Never give in.
Never. Never. Never.
Churchill's credo which is also Ross Perot's motto

Sometimes the good Lord has to hit us
with a sledgehammer to knock
some sense into our heads.

George Jones

Sometimes, bad is best.

Davy Crockett

No experience is a bad experience unless
you gain nothing from it.

Lyndon Baines Johnson

Failures that transform a businessman into
a super-cautious individual can cripple, and
this attitude has to be guarded against.

Trammell Crow

When I was a kid in Houston,
    we were so poor we couldn't afford the
    last two letters — we were just po!
George Foreman

A hungry dog hunts best.

Lee Trevino

You can't polish diamonds with velvet.

Zig Ziglar

There ain't a horse that can't be rode.
    There ain't a man that can't be throwed.
Saying of the Old West

Lord, don't remove any stumbling blocks.
Just give me strength.

Earl Campbell

Take your lies as they come.
Take the bad bounces with the good ones.

Ben Crenshaw

Defeat in this world is no disgrace if you
fought well and fought for the right thing.

Katherine Anne Porter

There's no better place than Texas to start over.

John Connally

6

Observations on Business

Texans have much to say about business. One Austin businessman, C. M. Rogers, marketed "Texas Boast Cards" in the 1950s. Rogers once wrote:

I'm sick and tired of Texas
And all its sorry soil.
I drill and drill for water
And don't get nothin' but oil.

With apologies to wildcatters everywhere, the following gems of wisdom come courtesy of men and women who know their business — and can probably teach the rest of us a few things about ours.

There is always a market for the best.

Stanley Marcus

The most important justification for
being in business is service to others.

Mary Kay Ash

If something is not working, change it.
It's up to your customer to fall in love
with your product, not you.

Tommy Tune

Make sure that your associates are
partners, and not employees. That way they
will always be working for you — or perhaps
it would be better to say, with you.

Trammell Crow

Do something. If it doesn't work,
do something else. No idea is too crazy.

Jim Hightower

The trouble with business is that everybody
expects you to find oil on the surface.
You've got to go deeper than that.

Hugh Roy Cullen

Eagles don't flock — you have to find them
one at a time.

Ross Perot

Once you get that first million,
the other ones come a whole lot easier.

John Mecom, Sr.

Money as money is nothing. It's just
something to make bookkeeping convenient.

H. L. Hunt

The secret to the oil business?
You have to be lucky.

H. L. Hunt

Luck has helped me every day of my life,
and I'd rather be lucky than smart because a
lot of smart people aren't eatin' right.

Sid Richardson

Flank the old wells and drill deeper.

Hugh Roy Cullen

My business philosophy? Don't be in too big a hurry, don't get excited, and don't lose your sense of humor. You can't be objective and emotional at the same time.

Sid Richardson

You can make money if you can find a need.

Hank Avery

The customer is the most important part
of any business.

Stanley Marcus

Don't second-guess the customer.

Tommy Tune

Remember a trade works two ways:
it has to please both sides. I never made a
trade where I couldn't go back and make a
second trade easier than the first.

Sid Richardson

Burn the text books — rely on instincts
and common sense.

Bill Hayden

Be willing to make decisions. Don't say,
"Ready - aim - aim - aim..." Be willing to fire.

T. Boone Pickens

A mediocre idea that generates enthusiasm
will go further than a great idea
that inspires no one.

Mary Kay Ash

How do you sell a car? Tell them what
they want to hear.

Red McCombs

Selling is my religion — and I don't intend
to be sacrilegious.

Stanley Marcus

There is not an American on earth but
what loves land.

Sam Houston

My real estate advice: buy all the valley
land you can as quickly as you can.

Lloyd Millard Bentsen

The best fertilizer for a piece of land is the
footprints of its owner.

Lyndon Baines Johnson

The more wells you drill, the greater chance
you have of finding oil.

H. L. Hunt

7

Politics

Politics are to Texas what bullfights are to Spain: messy, gruesome, and highly entertaining. The following observations on the sport of political science come courtesy of Texans who know how the game is played.

If you want to go into politics,
first get your name known.

Davy Crockett

I seldom think about politics
more than 18 hours a day.

Lyndon Baines Johnson

A politician ought to be born a foundling
and remain a bachelor.

Lady Bird Johnson

Working in Washington means that
you're trying to do the Lord's work
in the Devil's workshop.

Phil Gramm

No man who goes to Congress should use
anybody else's head, brain or mouth.
Congress is not a place for a man
with a master.

Maury Maverick

The stakes are too high for government
to be a spectator sport.

Barbara Jordan

What's good for America is good for Texas.

Phil Gramm

A people who value privilege above
principle will soon lose both.

Dwight D. Eisenhower

People, in the long run, are more likely
to promote peace than governments.

Dwight D. Eisenhower

Upon the subject of military despotism,
I have never hesitated to express my opinion,
for I consider it the source of all revolutions
and the slavery and ruin of free people.

Stephen F. Austin

The example of the Alamo should not be lost
to us. If a man will willingly lose his life for the
liberty of his people, certainly now a man
should be willing to lose his political life for
the things that are right and just.

Maury Maverick

The benefits of education and of useful
knowledge, generally diffused through
a community, are essential to the
preservation of a free government.

Sam Houston

The speed of the leader
      is the speed of the gang.

Mary Kay Ash

Leadership: the art of getting someone else
    to do something you want done
      because he wants to do it.

Dwight D. Eisenhower

You cannot be a leader, and ask other people
    to follow you, unless you know
      how to follow, too.

Sam Rayburn

Remember loyalty is a two-way street.

Barbara Bush

The only things in the middle of the road are yellow stripes and dead armadillos.

Jim Hightower

The hardest task is not to do what is right
but to know what is right.

Lyndon Baines Johnson

You cannot change people's hearts merely
by changing the law.

Dwight D. Eisenhower

Democracy is liberty plus economic security.
We Americans want to pray, think as
we please — and eat regular.

Maury Maverick

Politics ought to be the part-time profession
of every citizen.

Dwight D. Eisenhower

8

Cities and Towns

Wichita Falls choreographer Tommy Tune once observed that, "Every Texas town has its profile." From the largest urban centers to the tiniest hamlets, Texas towns have personality.

In 1940, the Federal Writer's Program chronicled the Lone Star State. Despite numerous writers and substantial resources, that text began with these cautioning words: "Few men have seen all of Texas, and no visitor can hope to do so." So much for a comprehensive profile of every town in Texas.

The following quotations give us a sampling of a few Lone Star cities and villages. Further research is up to you.

Why would I want to live anywhere else but Texas, and in Center? It's the center of the universe. And I think it's the best.

Mattie Dellinger

I never found a place where I wanted to live more than Alvin.

Nolan Ryan

I'm glad I grew up in Lewisville. Small towns give you something big towns don't. You have time to enjoy life more.

Walt Garrison

There is no place quite like Abbott. That is where my dreams began, and I go back there to begin dreaming again, like a child ....

Willie Nelson

My favorite place in Texas is Lubbock. Mostly because Lubbock, like Popeye the Sailor, is what it is.

Molly Ivins

Presidio is the unadorned meeting place of two great nations.

James Michener

Amarillo is the place where
the rain is all wind and the wind is all sand.
Early German Settler

I'll always be an Aggie. Just don't ask me
to go back there and live.
Bear Bryant

Austin is the big middle of that enormous
quality called Texas.
Mary Lasswell

Austin: City of a Violet Crown.
O. Henry

Throughout San Antonio lingers the
influence of the conquistadors, the padres,
and the early Spanish settlers.
Federal Writer's Project

San Antonio is the most Roman Catholic,
and maybe the most cosmopolitan city
in America. European visitors
feel at home right away.
Insight Guides: Texas

In the daytime, San Antonio is more Mexican
than American, not quite genuine Mexican,
but picture postcard Mexican.
Graham Greene

El Paso. The border.
Here is a place all its own.

Insight Guides: Texas

El Paso— the city of the four Cs:
Climate, Cotton, Cattle, Copper.

John Gunther

Laredo is the most festive area along the
border. Washington's birthday and Mexican
Independence Day are celebrated with equal
fervor on both sides of the border.

Texas Handbook

Laredo – a respectable frontiertown.

Paul Theroux

Unlike some other Texas cities, Dallas has
no history of wild days. It came into
existence as a serious community with
citizens of a peaceable and cultured type.

Federal Writer's Project

Dallas is a city of sophistication.

Tommy Tune

Dallas and Fort Worth, separated by 30 miles
of suburbs, may be the oddest couple of all
in a state of odd couples.

Fodor's Travel Guidebook

Houston is, without a doubt, the weirdest, most entertaining city in Texas, consisting as it does of subtropical forest, life in the fast lane, a layer of oil, cowboys, and spacemen.

Insight Guides: Texas

I feel safer on a racetrack than I do on Houston's expressways.

A. J. Foyt

9

Attitude

The Roman poet Virgil lived over 2,000 years ago. Fully nineteen centuries before the advent of modern psychology, he realized the important role that a person's outlook plays in a happy and productive life. Virgil wrote, "They are able who think they are able." These eight words seem to sum up the can-do mind-set of the Lone Star State.

Virgil never made it to Texas, and that's too bad. With his attitude, he'd have made one heck of a good Texan.

Have faith.
It's contagious.

Sam Rayburn

When I started counting my blessings,
my whole life turned around.

Willie Nelson

When it gets right down to the woodchopping,
the key to winning is confidence.

Darrell Royal

It's a circle. Work and confidence.
And more work and more confidence.

Roger Staubach

Morale is the greatest single factor
in successful wars.

Dwight D. Eisenhower

You can't have a long, successful career
without a positive attitude.
A can-do mentality is a pitcher's best friend.

Nolan Ryan

Form a battle plan, gather your men
and equipment, and attack.
You have only one thought in mind:
you do whatever it takes to win.

Red Adair

Failure? I think failure is quitting.

John Connally

It ain't over till the fat lady sings.

Dan Cook

Pain comes like the weather,
　　　　　but joy is a choice.
Rodney Crowell

We create our own unhappiness.
　　The purpose of suffering is to help us
understand we are the ones who cause it.
Willie Nelson

Accomplishment is 85 percent attitude
　　　　and 15 percent skill.
Zig Ziglar

If your mind determines that something
　　shall be, your body will surprise you in
　　　the way it bucks up and behaves.
Katherine Stinson

Too much self-pity
will give you a
nervous breakdown.

Sid Richardson

10

Success and Failure

Who is the greatest female athlete in history? Many vote for Babe Didrikson Zaharias, a native of Beaumont. After winning Olympic gold in track and field, Babe went on to have a remarkable career in professional golf. She possessed great natural talent but nevertheless practiced diligently to hone her skills.

What inner motives drove Babe to the top? She once remarked, "I've always had the urge to do things better than anybody else." Spoken like a true Texan.

S uccess is doing something you love
and doing it well.

Ross Perot

W e succeed only as we identify in life, or in
war, or in anything else, a single overriding
objective, and make all other considerations
bend to that one objective.

Dwight D. Eisenhower

I black things out, focusing
on the task at hand.

Nolan Ryan

T o begin with, you must know what you want.

Mary Kay Ash

I never had the ambition
to be something.
I had the ambition
to do something.

Walter Cronkite

Pride. I need no one to inspire me. It's not up
to anyone else to make me give my best.

Hakeem Olajuwon

I know the secret to success.
It is my friend, discipline.

Bella Karolyi

Predictability can lead to failure.

T. Boone Pickens

Y̶ou shouldn't change what you are
in the search for success.

Sissy Spacek

Y̶ou do not create a style.
You work and develop yourself; your style is an
emanation from your own being.

Katherine Anne Porter

O̶ne of the first things my mother taught me
when I started playing in public was, "You
must make it look easy, whether it is or not."

Van Cliburn

Ideas are a dime a dozen. People who implement them are priceless. Nothing great is ever accomplished without follow-through.

Mary Kay Ash

It's a lot easier to stay interested and
motivated when you're winning.

Gordon Wood

Winning isn't getting ahead of others — it's
getting ahead of yourself.

Roger Staubach

Tomorrow is ours to win or to lose.

Lyndon Baines Johnson

There is a proud undying thought in man,
that bids his soul look upward
to fame's proud cliff!

Sam Houston

Don't be afraid to give up the good
to go for the great.

Kenny Rogers

We must carry with us the old virtues that
we have needed on every frontier: courage,
faith in God, honesty, eagerness to work hard.

Lyndon Baines Johnson

Once you replace negative thoughts
with positive ones, you'll start
having positive results.

Willie Nelson

The secret to winning is
constant, consistent management.

Tom Landry

People fail forward to success.

Mary Kay Ash

The world doesn't care why you can't get the job done. It only pays off on results.

Bum Bright

The greatest toll gate is that of success.

Texas Guinan, Entertainer

People always ask me if success is going to change me, and I tell them I sure hope so.

Randall "Tex" Cobb

Be brave if you lose
and meek if you win.

Harvey Penick

We must exchange the philosophy of excuse for the philosophy of responsibility.

Barbara Jordan

11

Courage

Texas is a state born of courage. Names like Austin, Crockett, Travis and Bowie have come to symbolize bravery and backbone.

Sam Houston's friend and mentor, Andrew Jackson, said, "One man with courage is a majority." Houston needed those words on a day in 1836 when he led 743 men against a Mexican army twice that size. On the bank of the San Jacinto, Houston's troops routed the enemy. Santa Anna was captured and Texas independence was secure.

If one man with courage forms a majority, it's small wonder that 736 men with courage can form a nation.

Courage can achieve everything.

Sam Houston

The brave man is not he who feels no fear,
but rather is the man who subdues fear and
bravely encounters the danger.

Lorenzo de Zavala

What's gonna happen is gonna happen.
So why be afraid?

Bill Pickett

It's the price of leadership to do the thing
you believe has to be done at the time
it must be done.

Lyndon Baines Johnson

Don't ever underestimate
the heart of a champion.

Rudy Tomjanovich

Fear is either a lack of confidence
  or a lack of knowledge — which are both
  the same thing. You are afraid to attempt
  something you believe you cannot do.

Katherine Stinson

Do not be afraid to fail, and if you do fail,
  try again and again and again.

Bum Bright

The most difficult challenge to overcome —
  and the most important —
  is the fear of failure.

Bette Graham

Mountain-moving faith is not just dreaming
  and desiring. It is daring to risk failure.

Mary Kay Ash

Become so wrapped up
in something that
you forget to be afraid.

Lyndon Baines Johnson

You don't build character with somebody
slapping you around.

Tom Landry

Go right to the mat and fight to the finish.

Katherine Anne Porter

It's not just enough to swing at the ball.
You've got to loosen your girdle
and really let the ball have it.

Babe Didrikson Zaharias

My mother never warned me not to do this
or that for fear of being hurt. Of course
I got hurt, but I was never afraid.

Katherine Stinson

When you start worrying about mistakes
is when you start losing.

Roger Staubach

One of the marks
of a gift is to have the
courage to pursue it.

Katherine Anne Porter

It's how you show up
at the showdown
that counts.

Homer Norton

12

Life

Texas has more than its share of porch-swing philosophers. Colorful men and women from all walks of life have commented on the human condition. The world as seen from the Lone Star State is most often pleasant, seldom regrettable, never hopeless. Even the bad times contain more than a few blessings.

There's an old Texas saying: "Life ain't in holding a good hand, but in playing a poor one well." The following observations will help you play *your* cards well, whether you're holding a pair of deuces or a handful of aces.

Life is like a layer cake. You just put one layer on top of the other, and whether you frost it or not is up to you.

Ann Richards

Life is facing challenges, going through
them and getting to the other side.

D. D. Lewis

Life's sands run fast.

Sam Houston

The awards and championships are great,
but the journey is what I'll remember.

Hakeem Olajuwon

We can draw from the past,
but we cannot live in it.

Lyndon Baines Johnson

You can't enjoy true freedom without limits.

Tom Landry

Freedom must be earned daily.

Dwight D. Eisenhower

A man can exist in his shell for a lifetime,
but if there is anything in the world
worth living for, it is freedom.

Davy Crockett

Most people live and die with their music
  still unplayed. They never dare to try.

Mary Kay Ash

You have to live through life's experiences of
heartache, sorrow, troubles, and sadness.
Then you can sing a sad song.

George Jones

My guitar is half my life,
  and my wife is the other half.

Leadbelly

First become a winner in life. Then it's easier
  to become a winner on the field.

Tom Landry

You can't wait on life.
If you do, you're living
some life that's
"gonna happen"
instead of the one that's
happening right now.

Ann Richards

All our lives we
are preparing to be
something or somebody,
even if we don't know it.

Katherine Anne Porter

Life consists of a lot
of minor annoyances
and a few matters
of real consequence.

Harvey Penick

13

Work

Texans appreciate the value of a hard day's work. Golfer Ben Hogan was asked why he worked so relentlessly on the practice tee. He responded, "Every day you don't practice is another day longer that it takes to be good."

The following insights extol the dignity, the rewards, and the pleasures of an honest day's work — Lone Star style.

Don't fear your job. Respect it.

Red Adair

Don't expect financial rewards to come
quickly or easily. It took me 15 years
to build up an income that exceeded
our family's monthly needs.

Ross Perot

Spectacular achievements are always
preceded by unspectacular preparation.

Roger Staubach

Texas Wisdom

If I've learned one thing in life,
     it's that hard work pays off.

Phil Gramm

What makes a good actor?
    Desire is the first ingredient. Hard work
    follows desire, and the motivation to do
    something about it all day, every day.

Tommy Lee Jones

There are no obstacles that hard work and
    preparation cannot cure.

Barbara Jordan

My mother taught me that hard work is a real virtue and that it can also be lots of fun.

Ann Richards

People who learn to be service oriented actually derive more pleasure from their work.

Stanley Marcus

My work? I'm makin' people happy, and they darn sure make me happy.

George Jones

If you're dedicated, if it's something that lives and breathes in your heart, then you've simply got to go ahead and do it.

Rodney Crowell

When you are in any contest, you should
work as if there were, up to the very
last minute, a chance to lose it.
This is battle, this is politics,
this is anything.

Dwight D. Eisenhower

The only discipline that lasts is self-discipline.

Bum Phillips

Discipline, the guardian of the state.

Motto of the University of Texas

My philosophy? Practice, practice, practice — and win.

Babe Didrikson Zaharias

You've got to practice every day.
One day of practice is like one day of clean
living. It doesn't do you any good.

Abe Lemons

Some night I'll go home and pass away.
But I'll have spent my whole day at the office.

Trammell Crow

Don't tell me I'm too old. I got nine kids.
I gotta work till I can't work no more.

George Foreman

When the work is done, there's time enough
for blowin' your own horn.

Sam Rayburn

Luck is what happens
when preparation meets
opportunity.

Darrell Royal

14

Texas Independence

Texas became an independent nation in 1836. It voluntarily joined the Union of the United States of America in 1845. The spirit of Texas independence is alive and well today. The following quotations serve as a reminder of the men and women who fought to earn and preserve that freedom.

The province of Techas will be the
richest state of our Union without a doubt.

Thomas Jefferson in a letter to James Monroe, 1820

The first colony of foreigners or Americans
ever settled in Texas was by myself.

Stephen F. Austin

No frontiersman who has no other
occupation than that of hustler
will be received — no drunkard,
no gambler, no profane swearer, no idler.

Stephen F. Austin's rules for his outpost

I have seen several friends here lately from
Texas. All represent that it is a lovely region!

Sam Houston, Nashville, 1832

As my country no longer needs my services,
I have made up my mind to go to Texas.

Davy Crockett
After losing a congressional election in Tennessee

G. T. T.
(Gone to Texas)
18th and 19th century slang phrase

If Mexico takes no steps to check this
   change, the province of Texas will very
shortly cease to belong to that government.
                              Alexis de Tocqueville

I have sworn to be a good Texan, and that
   I will not forswear. I will die for that which I
firmly believe for I know it is just and right.
One life is a small price for a cause so great.
                              José Antonio Navarro

War in defense of our rights is inevitable
in Texas. If volunteers from the United States
   will join their brethren in this section,
      they will receive liberal bounties.
                              Sam Houston

Texas could get along
without the United States,
but the United States
cannot, except at great
hazard, exist
without Texas.

Sam Houston

Injustice will, in the end, produce independence.

Lorenzo de Zavala

The people of Texas are informed that their
fellow citizens at Gonzales have been attacked.
The war has commenced.

Stephen F. Austin

Texas shall be free and independent,
or we shall perish with glory in battle.

Juan N. Seguin

Let the love of freedom and the love of liberty
drive us to the eventual free Republic of Texas.

Lorenzo de Zavala

I shall never surrender or retreat.

William B. Travis, at the Alamo

I am determined to sustain myself as long as possible and die like a soldier who never forgets what is due his honor and that of his country. Victory or Death.

William B. Travis

Pop, pop, pop! Bom, bom, bom! Throughout the day — no time for memorandums now. Go ahead. Liberty and independence forever.

Davy Crockett

Last entry in his journal, The Alamo, March 5, 1836

This day, Palm Sunday, March 7th, has been to me a day of heartfelt sorrow. At six in the morning, the execution of American prisoners was commenced. The stones of the earth seemed to cry out in compassion.

Commander of firing squad
Mexican Officer, Massacre of Goliad, 1836

The victims of the Alamo, and the names of those who were massacred at Goliad, call for cool, deliberate vengeance.

Sam Houston to his troops, April 7, 1836

Remember the Alamo!

Battle cry of the army of Texas, 1836

Sir: I have kept the army together under
most discouraging circumstances, and I hope
a just and wise God, in whom I have
always believed, will yet save Texas.

Sam Houston to David G. Burnet, April 6, 1836

The fierce vengeance of Texas
could not be resisted.

Sam Houston

Description of the triumph over Santa Anna
at the Battle of San Jacinto, April 21, 1836

It is our Alamo — and how do we treat it?
How can we expect others to attach the
importance to it that it so well deserves
when we Texans don't? The Alamo should
stand out free and clear. All unsightly
obstructions should be torn away.

Clara Driscoll

The prosperity of Texas has been the object
of my labors, the idol of my existence.

Stephen F. Austin
His self-styled epitaph, December 27, 1836

My great desire is that our country,
Texas, shall be annexed to the United States.

Sam Houston
President of Texas, in a confidential letter to his old friend,
Andrew Jackson, President of the United States

Man and woman were not more formed
for union, by the hand of God, than Texas
and the United States are formed
for union by the hand of nature.

Dollar Globe, 1844

The Lone Star of Texas has culminated and
passed on and become forever fixed in that
glorious Constellation, The American Union.
The Republic of Texas is no more.

Anso Jones, Last President of Texas, February 19, 1846

15

Observations on Texas Cuisine, Texas Mornings, Texas Football and Other Necessities of Life

We close with an assortment of observations from and about Texas. Enjoy.

Go West, young, man and grow up with the country.

Horace Greeley

Public Notice:
Any person caught
monkeying with my cattle
without permission
will catch Hell.

Yours in Christ,
Grizzley Calleen

Notice in Tescosa Pioneer, September 29, 1886

For the real taste of Texas, try barbecue, chicken-fried steak and Tex-Mex food. All are hearty, tasty and inexpensive.

From The Texas Monthly Guidebook to Texas

Texas Wisdom

No one has a finer command
of the language than the person
who keeps his mouth shut.

Sam Rayburn

Timing is everything. Bob Hope owns
most of Palm Springs because he knows
when not to say anything.

Ann Richards

I don't go by "the book." I've never seen
the book. I don't know who wrote it.
Until I get my hands on it, I'll keep
on using my own common sense.

Bum Phillips

Guys who think too much about the future
end up layin' on the canvas sayin',
"Where am I?"

George Foreman

A town that can't support one lawyer
    can always support two.

Lyndon Baines Johnson

A familiar acquaintance with the work
    of God is worth more than
    all the wisdom of the schools.

Sam Houston

If you think you can, you can.
    And if you think you can't, you're right.

Mary Kay Ash

Negativism is nothing more than
    the improper use of your imagination.

Zig Ziglar

If you don't get up and
stir around in the morning,
you've missed the best
part of the day.

Watt Matthews

Any jackass can kick
down a barn, but it takes
a good carpenter
to build one.

Sam Rayburn

Men are born equal, free, and are
   distinguished alone by virtue.
                              Lorenzo de Zavala

Force begets force. Hatred begets hatred.
                              Maury Maverick

Poverty has many roots,
   but the tap root is ignorance.
                              Lyndon Baines Johnson

Through the light of knowledge,
   the people will find a way.
                  Motto of Texas College, Tyler, Texas

Don't try to go too fast. Learn your job.
Don't ever talk until you know
what you're talking about.

Sam Rayburn

Learning and devotion are vital.

Motto of Texas Wesleyan College

I don't mind people thinking I'm stupid,
but I don't want to give them any proof.

Bum Phillips

God does not ask your ability or inability.
He asks only your availability.

Mary Kay Ash

Discipline wins.

Bella Karolyi

Don't tell people what to do. The gifted
don't need it, and others can't take it.

Katherine Anne Porter

There's a lot more to this life
    than just the struggle to make money.

Ann Richards

The day I made Eagle Scout was
    more important to me than the day
    I discovered I was a billionaire.

Ross Perot

The question isn't at what age I want to retire,
    but at what income.

George Foreman

I hate it when people smoke right next to me!
Selena

On this planet, we will always know the
Athlete of Athletes is between 45 and 55.
George Foreman

Fame is like a shaved pig with a greased tail.
It is only after it's slipped through the
hands of thousands, that some fellow,
by mere chance, holds on to it.
Davy Crockett

While you're trying to save face,
you're probably losing your rear.
Lyndon Baines Johnson

Football is just more important here in Texas. It's a tradition; almost a heritage. A daddy played for Brownwood High, so his son is playing now, and in not too many years, his son will be playing. Yes, we take it seriously.

Gordon Wood

An atheist is a guy who watches the Notre Dame - SMU game and doesn't care who wins.

Dwight D. Eisenhower

Life really wouldn't be worth livin' if you didn't have high school football.

Bob Rutherford

At first glance, Texas A&M looked a lot like a penitentiary.

Bear Bryant

My favorite Aggie joke?
I'm sorry I don't
understand
the question.

Lyle Lovett

Class of 1979

Turn out the lights,
the party's over.

Don Meredith

Sources

Sources

About the Author

Criswell Freeman is a Doctor of Clinical Psychology living in Nashville, Tennessee. He is the author of *When Life Throws You a Curveball, Hit It* and *The Wisdom Series* from WALNUT GROVE PRESS. He is also a published country music songwriter.

Dr. Freeman is the proud grandson of Marie Tabler Freeman, a native of Royce City. Mrs. Freeman traces her Texas ancestry to the days of the Alamo. Although she has lived outside the state for over 80 years, Marie still considers herself a Texan.

The Wisdom Series
by Dr. Criswell Freeman

The Book of All American Wisdom
ISBN 0-9640955-2-1

The Book of Southern Wisdom
ISBN 0-9640955-3-X

The Book of Country Music Wisdom
ISBN 0-9640955-1-3

The Golfer's Book of Wisdom
ISBN 0-9640955-6-4

The Wisdom of Southern Football
ISBN 0-9640955-7-2

The Book of Texas Wisdom
ISBN 0-9640955-8-0

The Book of Florida Wisdom
ISBN 0-9640955-9-9

Wisdom Books are available through
booksellers everywhere. For information about
a retailer near you, call 1-800-256-8584.